layTime Piano

Christmas

P9-DGI-957

Level 1

5-Finger Melodies

This book belongs to: _____

Arranged by

Nancy and Randall Faber

Production: Frank and Gail Hackinson
Production Coordinators: Satish Bhakta and Marilyn Cole
Design: Terpstra Design, San Francisco
Engraving: Tempo Music Press, Inc.
Printer: Tempo Music Press, Inc.

THE
F·J·H
MUSIC
COMPANY
INC.

Frank J. Hackinson

2525 Davie Road, Suite 360
Fort Lauderdale, Florida 33317-7424

A NOTE TO TEACHERS

PlayTime® Piano Christmas is a collection of favorite Christmas songs arranged for the beginning pianist. For special student appeal, the book features both the well-known Christmas carols and the popular Christmas favorites.

The arrangements use primarily 5-finger hand positions for simplicity, yet extend enough beyond middle C position to reinforce note reading and interval recognition.

PlayTime® Piano Christmas is part of the *PlayTime® Piano* series arranged by Faber and Faber. "PlayTime" designates Level 1 of the *PreTime® to BigTime® Supplementary Library*, and it is available in a variety of styles including Children's Songs, Christmas, Classics, Favorites, Hymns, Jazz & Blues, Popular, More Popular, and Rock 'n Roll.

Following are the levels of the supplementary library which lead up to *BigTime®.*

PreTime® Piano	(Primer Level)
PlayTime® Piano	(Level 1)
ShowTime® Piano	(Level 2A)
ChordTime® Piano	(Level 2B)
FunTime® Piano	(Level 3A – 3B)
BigTime® Piano	(Level 4)

Each level offers books in a variety of styles, making it possible for the teacher to offer stimulating material for every student. For a complimentary detailed listing, write the publisher listed below.

Teacher Duets

Optional teacher duets are a valuable feature of the *PlayTime® Piano* series. Although the arrangements stand complete on their own, the duets provide additional fullness of harmony and rhythmic vitality. And not incidentally, they offer the opportunity for parent and student to play together.

Helpful Hints:

1. The student should know his or her part thoroughly before the teacher duet is used. Accurate rhythm is especially important.

2. Harmony notes in the student part may be omitted if a steady rhythm is difficult to achieve.

3. Rehearsal numbers are provided to give the student and teacher starting places.

4. The teacher may wish to count softly a measure before beginning, as this will help the ensemble.

ISBN 0-929666-02-X

Copyright © 1988 by THE FJH MUSIC COMPANY INC. (ASCAP).
2525 Davie Road, Suite 360, Fort Lauderdale, Florida 33317-7424
International Copyright Secured.   All Rights Reserved.   Printed in U.S.A.

TABLE OF CONTENTS

Jingle Bells 4

O Come, All Ye Faithful (Adeste Fideles) 6

When Santa Claus Gets Your Letter 8

Silent Night 10

Away in a Manger 12

The First Noel 13

Joy to the World 14

Rudolph the Red-Nosed Reindeer 16

A Holly Jolly Christmas 18

The Night Before Christmas Song 20

Rockin' Around the Christmas Tree 22

We Wish You a Merry Christmas 24

Music Dictionary 25

4

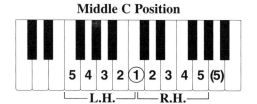

Middle C Position

Jingle Bells

Words and Music by
J. PIERPONT

With excitement

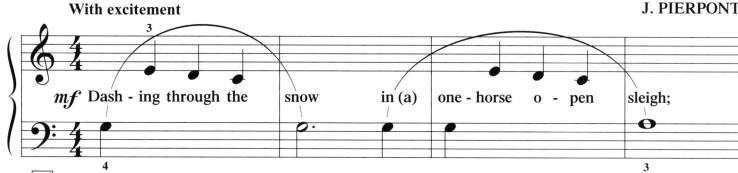

mf Dash - ing through the snow in (a) one - horse o - pen sleigh;

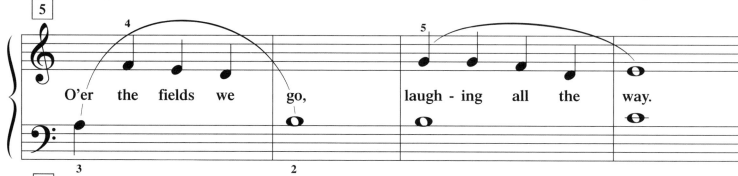

O'er the fields we go, laugh - ing all the way.

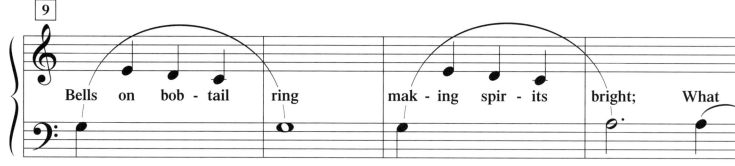

Bells on bob - tail ring mak - ing spir - its bright; What

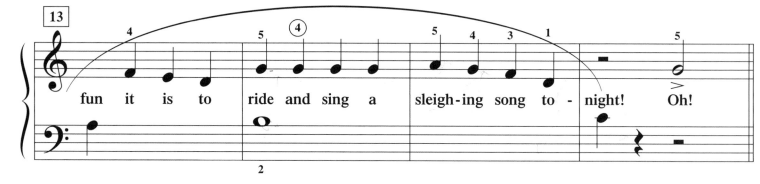

fun it is to ride and sing a sleigh-ing song to - night! Oh!

Teacher Duet: (Student plays 1 octave higher)

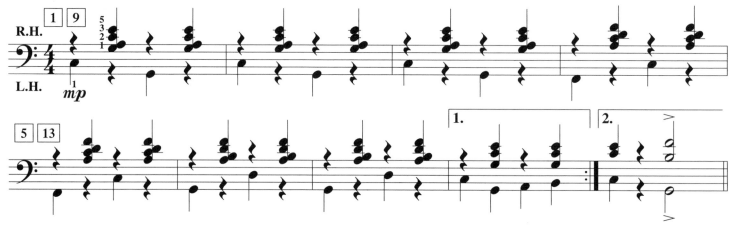

Middle C Position

O Come, All Ye Faithful
(Adeste Fideles)

Transcribed by F. OAKELEY
WADE'S "CANTUS DIVERSI"

Boldly

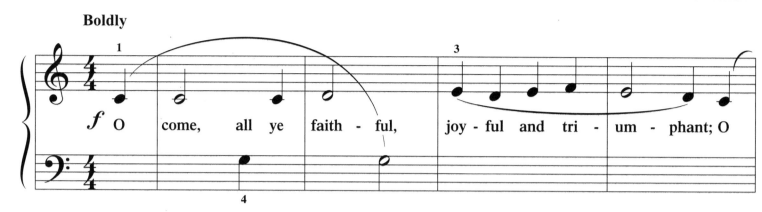

O come, all ye faith - ful, joy - ful and tri - um - phant; O

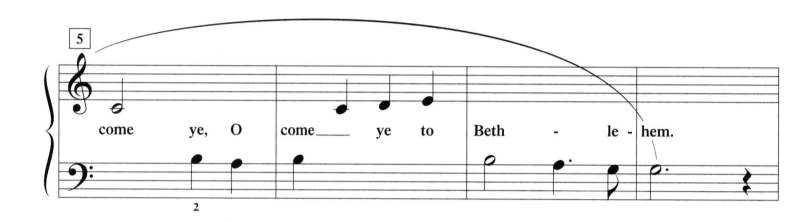

come ye, O come ___ ye to Beth - le - hem.

Teacher Duet: (Student plays 1 octave higher)

Come and be - hold Him, Born the King of an - gels. O *p*

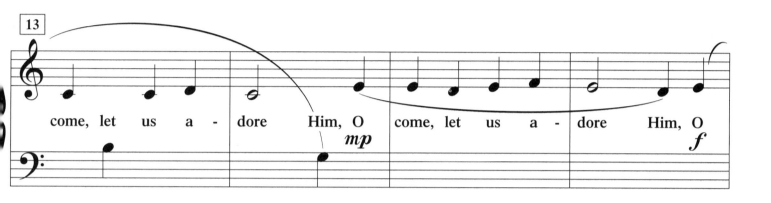

come, let us a - dore Him, O *mp* come, let us a - dore Him, O *f*

come, let us a - dore Him,___ Christ,___ the Lord.

8

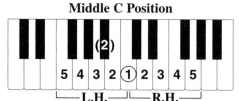

Middle C Position

When Santa Claus Gets Your Letter

Music and Lyrics by
JOHNNY MARKS

Teacher Duet: (Student plays 1 octave higher)

DEC 8

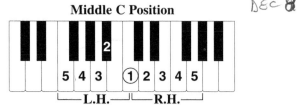

Silent Night

Words by JOSEPH MOHR
Music by FRANZ GRÜBER

Peacefully

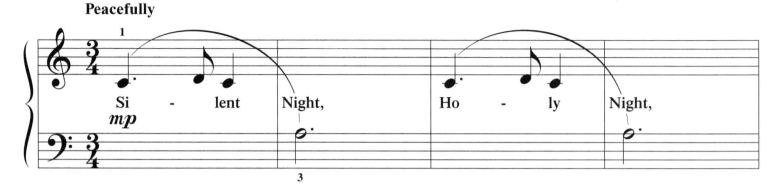

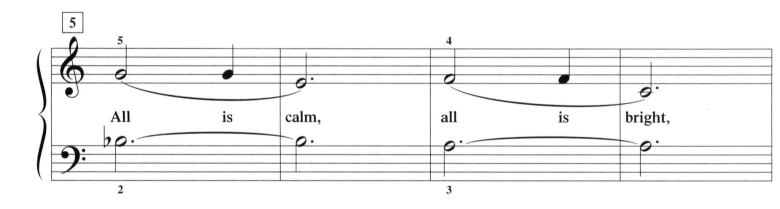

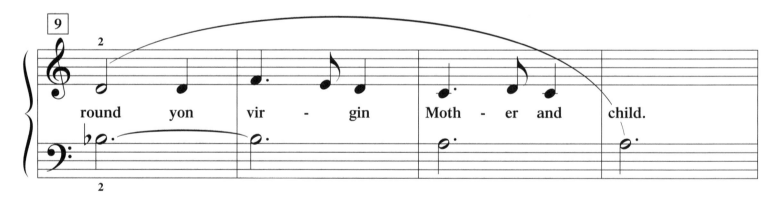

Teacher Duet: (Student plays 1 octave higher)

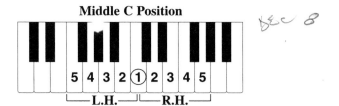

DEC 8

Away in a Manger

JAMES R. MURRAY
Traditional

Gently

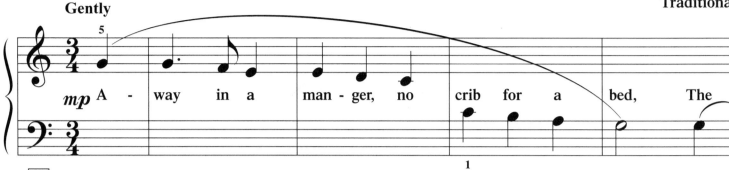

mp A - way in a man - ger, no crib for a bed, The

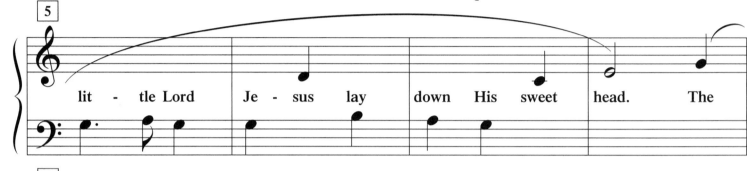

lit - tle Lord Je - sus lay down His sweet head. The

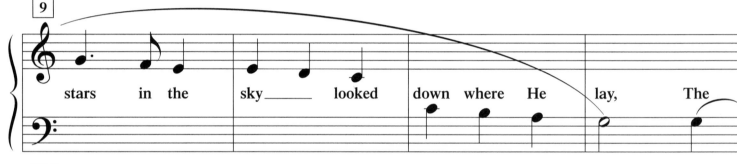

stars in the sky____ looked down where He lay, The

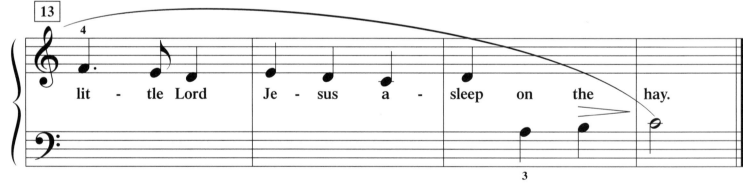

lit - tle Lord Je - sus a - sleep on the hay.

Teacher Duet: (Student plays 1 octave higher)

Middle C Position

DEC 8

The First Noel

TRADITIONAL

Teacher Duet: (Student plays 1 octave higher)

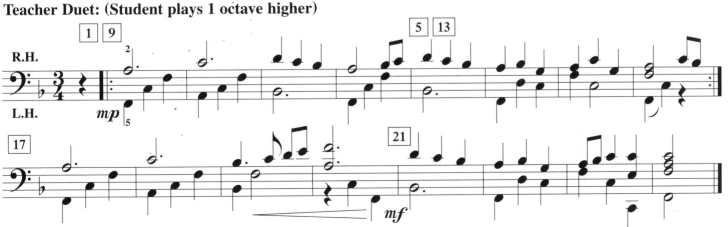

14

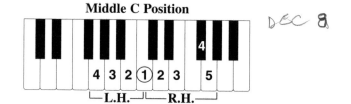

DEC 8

Joy to the World

Words by ISAAC WATTS
Music by G.F. HANDEL

Joyfully

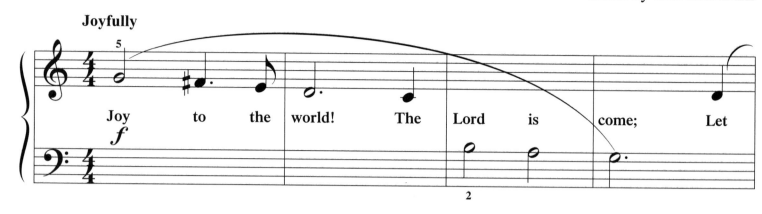

Joy   to   the   world!   The   Lord   is   come;   Let

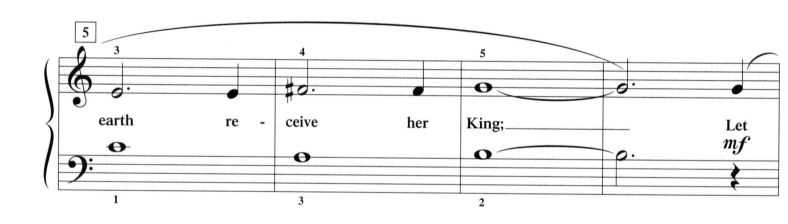

earth   re - ceive   her   King;_____   Let

Teacher Duet: (Student plays 1 octave higher)

FF1002

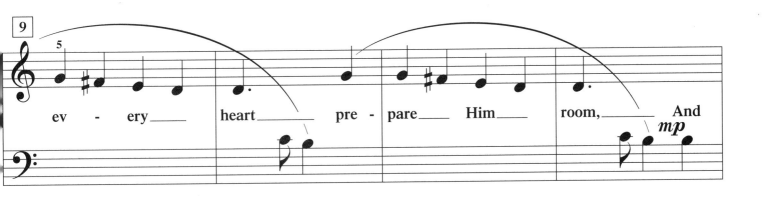

Rudolph the Red-Nosed Reindeer

Music and Lyrics by
JOHNNY MARKS

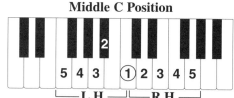

Teacher Duet: (Student plays 1 octave higher)

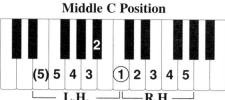

A Holly Jolly Christmas

**Music and Lyrics by
JOHNNY MARKS**

Teacher Duet: (Student plays 1 octave higher)

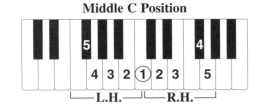

The Night Before Christmas Song

Music by JOHNNY MARKS
Lyric adapted by JOHNNY MARKS
From Clement Moore's Poem

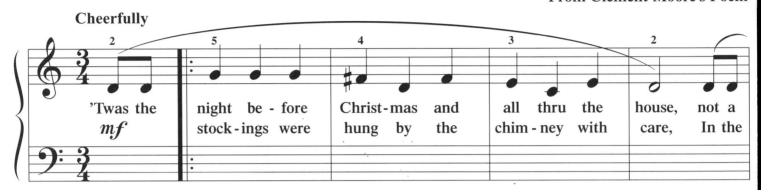

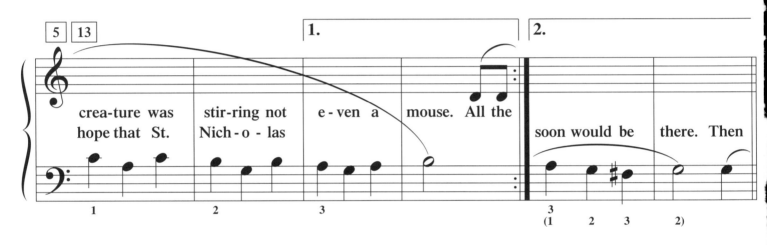

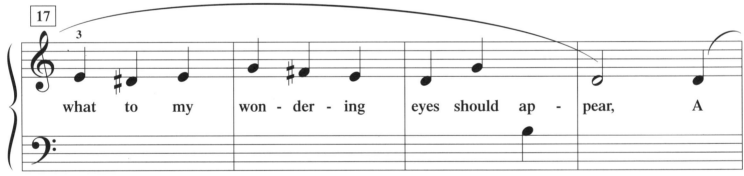

Teacher Duet: (Student plays 1 octave higher)

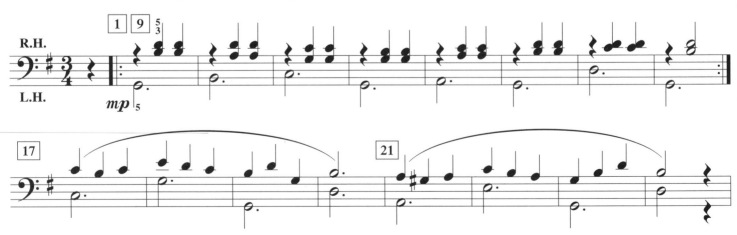

Rockin' Around The Christmas Tree

Music and Lyrics by
JOHNNY MARKS

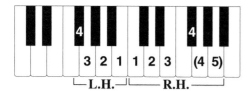

With a great beat

Rock-in' a - round the Christ-mas tree at the Christ-mas par - ty hop.

Mis-tle-toe hung where you can see every cou - ple tries to stop.

Rock-in' a - round the Christ-mas tree let the Christ-mas spir - it ring.

Lat-er we'll have some pun - kin pie and (we'll) do some car - ol - ing.

Teacher Duet: (Student plays 1 octave higher)

To Coda

We Wish You a Merry Christmas

TRADITIONAL ENGLISH CAROL

FF1002